CW00369805

bite-s

Thai

First published in 2000 by Hamlyn
an imprint of Octopus Publishing Group Limited
2–4 Heron Quays
London E14 4JP

Copyright © 2000 Octopus Publishing Group Limited

All rights reserved. No part of this publication may be
reproduced, stored in a retrieval system, or transmitted,
in any form or by any means, electronic, electrostatic,
magnetic tape, mechanical, photocopying, recording
or otherwise without the prior permission in writing of the
publisher.

British Library Cataloguing-in-Publication Data
A catalogue record for this book is available from the British
Library

ISBN 0 600 60148 X

Produced by Toppan
Printed in China

Managing Editor: Clare Johnson
Editor: Anne Crane
Proofreader: Claire Hacking
Indexer: Diana LeCore
Creative Director: Keith Martin
Designer: David Godfrey
Production Controller: Lisa Moore

Notes

Standard level spoon measurements are used in all recipes
1 tablespoon = one 15 ml spoon
1 teaspoon = one 5 ml spoon

Both imperial and metric measurements have been given in all recipes.
Use one set of measurements only and not a mixture of both.

Eggs should be medium unless otherwise stated.

Milk should be full fat unless otherwise stated.

Pepper should be freshly ground black pepper unless otherwise stated.

Fresh herbs should be used unless otherwise stated. If unavailable use
dried herbs as an alternative but halve the quantities stated.

Oven should be preheated to the specified temperature – if using a
fan assisted oven, follow the manufacturer's instructions for adjusting
the time and temperature.

Thai cooks rarely deseed chillies (the seeds and surrounding membrane
are the hottest part). If you prefer a milder flavour, remove the seeds
before use.

bite-sized
Thai

contents

or a spoon and fork to eat with, except for noodles which are eaten with chop-sticks. Knives are not used at table.

Thai street food is world-renowned. The street vendors, who are found in huge numbers in all the cities, specialize in one item or dish – they may have a stall at a street market or be perpetually on the move, complete with their cooking equipment, hawking their wares from trays hanging from a yoke, a wheeled handcart or a trolley. Selling between them an immense range of tantalizing snacks both hot and cold, at a fraction of restaurant prices, they are immensely and deservedly popular.

Because of its informal style, Thai food adapts perfectly to picnics, drinks parties, light lunches and in fact to feeding friends and family on all the occasions when you want an appetizing snack or series of snacks rather than a formal meal.

The only equipment you need to cook in Thai style is a wok, a steamer and a food processor or pestle and mortar for chop-ping and grinding. The enormous and growing popularity of Thailand, for both package tourists and backpackers, and the rapidly increasing number of Thai restaurants across the globe means that Thai food becomes steadily easier to find in supermarkets and oriental stores. The ingredients needed to make a simple curry paste, for example, are increasingly familiar. The glossary on pages 8–9 describes any unusual ingredients you will need to cook the recipes in this book.

glossary

Basil

Holy basil is as common in Thai cooking as sweet basil is in Europe. Although holy basil has a smaller darker leaf and purple stalks, its flavour is similar to sweet basil.

Bean thread noodles

These noodles, which are made from mung beans, are also known as glass noodles, cellophane noodles and bean vermicelli.

Chillies

Introduced by the Portuguese in the 16th century, these are used in very large quantities in Thailand. Green chillies are generally hotter than red chillies and dried ones are hotter than fresh, with the seeds being the hottest part of all. Take care when preparing chillies; wear rubber gloves if your hands are sensitive and do not touch your face, particularly your eyes, until you have washed your hands.

Coconut milk

This is widely available in cans, blocks and packets. You can also make your own using dessicated coconut. The recipe is on page 79.

Coriander

An essential ingredient in Thai cooking. All parts of the plant are used – leaves, stems, roots and seeds.

Galangal

A root very similar to ginger, which can be used instead. Ground galangal is sold as laos powder.

Glutinous rice

A variety of short-grain rice, essential for cooking Thai sticky rice (see page 79).

Ground dried shrimp

A very pungent flavouring found all over South-East Asia. Once opened, it should be stored in a jar with a tightly-fitting lid.

Lemon grass

A highly aromatic plant with a strong lemon flavour and fragrance. The long, tapering stems, which are quite substantial, are added to curries, soups and curry pastes and even used as kebab skewers. Fresh lemon grass is sold in bunches of 6–8 stalks in supermarkets and oriental stores. Dried powdered lemon grass, known as serai, can be found in oriental stores.

Lime leaves

Also known as kaffir lime leaves, these distinctively flavoured leaves can be found fresh and dried in oriental stores.

Nam pla

Also known as Thai fish sauce and fish gravy, this pungent bottled sauce is made from salted anchovies. It is widely used in Thai cooking to accentuate the taste of other foods, rather than to give a fishy flavour.

Oil

Groundnut oil is the most suitable for Thai cooking, although corn oil or vegetable oil can also be used. Olive oil has too distinctive a flavour.

Oyster sauce

A thick, salty brown condiment made from oysters and soy sauce.

Palm sugar

A soft, raw, light brown sugar which is used all over South-East Asia. Firmly packed light brown sugar can be used instead.

Soy sauce

This sauce, which is made from fermented soya beans, comes in light and dark varieties. The light salty variety is used in chicken and stir-fried rice dishes. The dark version which is less salty but thicker and sweeter is most often used in noodle dishes.

Spring roll wrappers

White, flimsy and fragile, these square pastry wrappers are available, fresh and frozen, from oriental stores. Filo pastry can be used as an alternative.

Tamarind

The fruit of a tropical tree used for its acidic flavour. Tamarind concentrate, which is dissolved in hot water, is simpler to use than dried tamarind pulp. Lemon juice or vinegar may be used as substitutes.

Turmeric

A mildly flavoured spice, usually sold powdered, which gives dishes a vivid yellow/orange colour.

Water chestnut

The core of a variety of water grass, water chestnuts have a very distinctive crunchy texture. Usually sold canned.

Wonton wrappers

Made from flour and eggs, these are deep yellow or brown in colour. They are sold ready-made, fresh and frozen in oriental shops.

nibbles

pork on pineapple

fried wonton with chilli sauce

steamed wonton

crispy wrapped prawns

toasted chilli cashews

thai prawn toasts

prawn and corn fritters

fried golden bags

crispy rice with dipping sauce

chillies stuffed with curried crab

deep-fried corn cakes

vegetables with coconut and yellow bean sauce

Serves 4 / **Preparation time** 15 minutes / **Cooking time** 20–25 minutes

pork on pineapple
mah hoh

- 3½ tablespoons vegetable oil
- ½ tablespoon chopped dried red chilli
- 1 tablespoon Garlic Mixture (see page 78)
- 125 g (4 oz) minced pork
- 125 g (4 oz) raw prawns, shelled, deveined and finely chopped
- 2 tablespoons nam pla (fish sauce)
- 2 tablespoons brown sugar
- 50 g (2 oz) peanuts, finely ground
- 1 large pineapple
- coriander leaves, to garnish

1   Heat ½ teaspoon of the oil in a small frying pan and fry the dried red chilli until crisp. Drain on kitchen paper.

2   Heat the remaining oil in a medium saucepan, add the garlic mixture and stir-fry for 2 minutes. Add the pork and prawns and cook for 5–6 minutes, stirring frequently to break up any lumps. Add the nam pla and sugar and cook for a further 10–15 minutes, stirring, until the mixture is thick and sticky.

3   Add the ground peanuts, stir well, and remove the pan from the heat.

4   Peel and core the pineapple and cut the flesh into 5 cm (2 inch) squares. Arrange the squares on a serving dish and top each one with 1 teaspoon of the pork mixture. Garnish with the coriander leaves and the fried chilli.

Variation This dish is equally good with oranges instead of pineapple. Peel and segment 6 oranges then, using a sharp knife, split each orange segment down the fleshy curve and open it out like a small pocket. Top with the pork mixture.

fried wonton with chilli sauce

geow grob

- **250 g (8 oz) minced pork**
- **1 tablespoon onion, finely chopped**
- **2 teaspoons Garlic Mixture (see page 78)**
- **½ tablespoon nam pla (fish sauce)**
- **20 wonton wrappers (suitable for frying)**
- **1 egg yolk, beaten**
- **oil, for deep-frying**
- **Chilli Sauce (see page 76) or Plum Sauce (see page 77), to serve**
- **1 spring onion, cut into very fine slivers, to garnish**

1　Put the minced pork into a small bowl with the chopped onion, garlic mixture and nam pla. Mix well to make a thick paste.

2　Spread out the wonton wrappers on a work surface and put a teaspoon of the pork mixture in the centre of each one. Brush the edges of the wrappers with the egg yolk then fold the wrappers over the filling to form triangles. Press the edges firmly together, sealing with more egg yolk if necessary.

3　Heat the oil in a wok and fry the filled wontons, a few at a time, for about 5 minutes, until they are golden brown. Turn them over in the oil if necessary so they are browned on both sides. Drain on kitchen paper and serve hot with chilli sauce or plum sauce, garnished with slivers of spring onion.

Serves 4–5 / **Preparation time** 15 minutes / **Cooking time** 20 minutes

steamed wonton

kanom jeeb

- **16 wonton wrappers**
- **oil, for drizzling**
- **Soy and Vinegar Dipping Sauce or Hot Sweet Sauce (see page 76), to serve**

FILLING

- **6 raw prawns, shelled**
- **125 g (4 oz) minced pork**
- **40 g (1½ oz) onion, chopped**
- **2 garlic cloves**
- **5 water chestnuts**
- **1 teaspoon palm sugar or soft brown sugar**
- **1 tablespoon light soy sauce**
- **1 egg**

1 To make the filling, blend all the ingredients in a food processor or blender.

2 Put 1 heaped teaspoon of the filling into the centre of a wonton wrapper, placed over your thumb and index finger. As you push the filled wrapper down through the circle your fingers form, tighten the top, shaping it but leaving the top open. Repeat this process with all the wrappers.

3 Put the filled wontons on to a plate and place the plate in a steamer. Drizzle a little oil on top of the wontons, put the lid on and steam for 30 minutes.

4 Serve the wontons hot or warm, with the dipping sauces served separately in bowls.

Serves 4 / **Preparation time** 15 minutes / **Cooking time** 30 minutes

crispy wrapped prawns

kung hom pa

- **75 g (3 oz) minced pork**
- **4 raw prawns, shelled and minced**
- **½ teaspoon sugar**
- **¼ onion, finely chopped**
- **1 garlic clove, finely chopped**
- **2 teaspoons light soy sauce**
- **12 raw prawns**
- **12 spring roll wrappers**
- **1 egg white, beaten**
- **oil, for deep-frying**
- **basil or coriander sprig, to garnish (optional)**
- **Hot Sweet Sauce (see page 76), to serve**

1   In a bowl, mix together the minced pork and prawns, sugar, onion, garlic and soy sauce and set aside.

2   Shell the other 12 raw prawns, leaving the tails intact, and carefully cut them open, making sure you do not cut right through them. Leave the shell-on tails uncut.

3   Put 1 teaspoon or more of the minced mixture on to each opened prawn. Take a spring roll wrapper and pull one corner about three-quarters of the way towards the opposite corner. Place a prawn on the double thickness of wrapper, leaving the tail free, and roll it up, tucking the ends in and sticking the wrapper down with a little egg white. Continue until all the prawns are wrapped.

4   Heat the oil in a wok and deep-fry the prawn rolls until golden – this should take about 5 minutes. Remove them from the wok with a slotted spoon and drain on kitchen paper. Garnish with a basil or coriander sprig, if wished, and serve with hot sweet sauce.

Makes 12 / **Preparation time** 20 minutes / **Cooking time** 5 minutes

toasted chilli cashews

pad med mamuang in mapan sai prik

- **250 g (8 oz) unsalted cashew nuts**
- **1 tablespoon groundnut oil**
- **1 garlic clove, finely chopped**
- **¼ teaspoon crushed dried chillies**
- **1 spring onion, finely chopped**
- **2 small fresh chillies (1 red, 1 green), finely chopped**
- **salt**

1 Put the nuts into a frying pan, without oil, and stir constantly until they turn golden. Remove from the heat and leave to cool.

2 In a wok, heat the oil and fry the garlic until golden brown. Add the cashews to the oil and sprinkle the crushed dried chillies over them. Stir-fry for 1 minute, then add the spring onion, chopped fresh chillies and salt to taste. Serve warm.

thai
prawn
toasts
kanam bung
nar gung

1 Put the minced prawns and pork into a bowl with the coriander leaves, spring onion, garlic mixture and nam pla. Add the egg and mix well.

2 Cut each slice of bread into 4 pieces of roughly equal size. Spread each piece of bread with the pork and prawn mixture, using a knife to press the mixture firmly on to the bread. Sprinkle the sesame seeds on top.

3 Pour about 2.5 cm (1 inch) of oil into a wok and heat to 180–190°C (350–375°F) or until a cube of bread browns in 30 seconds. Add the pieces of bread, a few at a time, with the topping side facing downwards. Cook over a moderate heat for 6–8 minutes, then turn over the bread and cook the other side until golden. Remove with a slotted spoon and drain on kitchen paper. Garnish with coriander and serve hot with plum sauce, very thin slices of green pepper and strips of mooli.

- **75 g (3 oz) uncooked prawns, peeled, deveined and minced**
- **125 g (4 oz) minced pork**
- **1 tablespoon coriander leaves, finely chopped, plus extra to garnish**
- **1 tablespoon finely chopped spring onion**
- **1 teaspoon Garlic Mixture (see page 78)**
- **1 tablespoon nam pla (fish sauce)**
- **1 egg, beaten**
- **5 slices white bread**
- **5 tablespoons sesame seeds**
- **vegetable oil for deep-frying**

TO SERVE
- **Plum Sauce (see page 77)**
- **¼ green pepper, very thinly sliced**
- **wide strips of raw mooli**

Tip Mooli comes from the same vegetable family as the radish, which can be used instead, but it is much larger and has a slightly less peppery taste.

Serves 4 / **Preparation time** 20 minutes / **Cooking time** 15–20 minutes

Serves 4-5 / **Preparation time** 5 minutes / **Cooking time** 10 minutes

prawn and corn fritters

tod mun kung

1 In a bowl, mix together the flour, minced prawns, red curry paste, sweetcorn kernels, egg white and kaffir lime leaf.

2 Heat the oil in a wok over a moderate heat, then add heaped tablespoons of the mixture and cook for about 5 minutes until golden brown. You may want to do this in batches.

3 Remove the fritters from the wok and drain on kitchen paper, then turn them on to a serving dish. Garnish with coriander, if using, and serve with the dipping sauces.

- **20 g (¾ oz) self-raising flour**
- **65 g (2½ oz) raw prawns, minced**
- **1 teaspoon Red Curry Paste (see page 78)**
- **50 g (2 oz) sweetcorn kernels**
- **1 egg white**
- **1 kaffir lime leaf, shredded**
- **oil, for deep-frying**
- **coriander sprigs, to garnish (optional)**

TO SERVE
- **Hot Sweet Sauce (see page 76)**
- **Soy and Vinegar Dipping Sauce (see page 76)**

fried golden bags

tang tong

- **20 wonton wrappers (suitable for frying)**
- **20 fresh flowering chives, about 10 cm (4 inches) long, plus extra to garnish**
- **oil, for deep-frying**

FILLING

- **75 g (3 oz) canned water chestnuts, chopped**
- **250 g (8 oz) crab meat**
- **50 g (2 oz) raw prawns, shelled and chopped**
- **2 teaspoons Garlic Mixture (see page 78)**
- **2 spring onions, chopped**
- **1 green chilli, deseeded and chopped**
- **1 tablespoon dark soy sauce**
- **1 tablespoon nam pla (fish sauce)**
- **Plum Sauce (see page 77) or Chilli Sauce (see page 76), to serve**

1 To make the filling, put all the ingredients into a large bowl and mix until thoroughly combined. You should end up with a thick paste.

2 Spread out the wonton wrappers on a work surface and divide the filling equally between them, putting a spoonful in the centre of each wrapper. Pull up the 4 corners into the middle to make little bags.

3 Using the chives, secure the little bags at the top. Take care that the chives do not break as you tie them.

4 Heat the oil in a wok or deep-fryer. Fry the little bags in batches, a few at a time, for 2–3 minutes until they are crisp and golden brown. Serve very hot with plum sauce or chilli sauce, garnished with a few of the extra chives.

Serves 4-5 / **Preparation time** 25 minutes / **Cooking time** 5-10 minutes

crispy rice with dipping sauce

khow tung nah tung

- **250 g (8 oz) glutinous rice**
- **vegetable oil, for deep-frying**

DIPPING SAUCE

- **125 ml (4 fl oz) coconut milk**
- **50 g (2 oz) minced pork**
- **50 g (2 oz) cooked, peeled prawns, minced**
- **1 teaspoon Garlic Mixture (see page 78)**
- **1½ teaspoons nam pla (fish sauce)**
- **1½ tablespoons sugar**
- **50 g (2 oz) onion, finely chopped**
- **50 g (2 oz) roasted peanuts, crushed (see page 77)**

1 Put the rice into a saucepan and pour in enough water to cover it. Bring to the boil, cover the pan and cook until the rice is thoroughly cooked and sticky. Drain the rice in a sieve then spread it out in as thin a layer as possible on greased baking trays, pressing down well. Set aside to dry in a warm place or in a preheated oven, 120°C (250°F), Gas Mark ½, for several hours or until completely dry and firm.

2 Meanwhile, make the dipping sauce. Pour the coconut milk into a saucepan and bring slowly to the boil. Add the minced pork and prawns, stirring to break up any lumps. Stir in the garlic mixture, nam pla, sugar, chopped onion and roasted peanuts then reduce the heat and simmer for 20 minutes, stirring occasionally.

3 When completely dry and firm, remove the rice pieces from the trays with a spatula, breaking them into large pieces.

4 Heat the oil for deep-frying to 180–190°C (350–375°F), or until a cube of bread browns in 30 seconds, and deep-fry the rice pieces until golden. You should hear the grains beginning to pop in about 5 seconds. Remove from the oil with a slotted spoon and drain on kitchen paper.

5 Pour the dipping sauce into a bowl and serve with the pieces of crispy rice.

Tip When boiling glutinous rice, Thai cooks reserve the layer of sticky grain left in the bottom of the saucepan to make this dish.

Serves 4 / **Preparation time** 10 minutes, + drying / **Cooking time** 25 minutes

chillies stuffed with curried crab

pik jut sigh pool

- **6 red jalapeño chillies**
- **6 green jalapeño chillies**
- **2 tablespoons vegetable oil**
- **2 garlic cloves, crushed**
- **1 teaspoon fresh root ginger, grated**
- **3 spring onions, chopped**
- **2 kaffir lime leaves, very finely chopped**
- **1 tablespoon Red Curry Paste (see page 78)**
- **¼ teaspoon turmeric**
- **150 g (5 oz) fresh or canned white crab meat, flaked**
- **1 tablespoon lime juice**
- **2 teaspoons nam pla (fish sauce)**

1 To prepare the chillies for stuffing, place them under a preheated hot grill and cook, turning occasionally, until they have softened and their skins are patched with black. This will take about 8–10 minutes.

2 Remove the chillies from the grill and leave them to cool, covered with sheets of dampened kitchen paper. (This makes them easier to peel once they have cooled.)

3 Meanwhile, prepare the stuffing. Heat the oil in a saucepan, add the garlic, ginger and spring onions and cook over a gentle heat for 3 minutes, until softened. Stir in the kaffir lime leaves, red curry paste and turmeric and cook, stirring, for a further 2 minutes. Remove the pan from the heat and stir in the flaked crab meat, lime juice and nam pla.

4 Peel the chillies, leaving the stalks intact, and make a slit down one side of each one from the stalk to the tip. Scrape out and discard the seeds. Stuff the chillies with the curried crab mixture then place them in a shallow oven-proof dish and cover them with foil.

5 Cook the chillies in a preheated oven, 200°C (400°F) Gas Mark 6, for 15 minutes until they are heated through. Serve immediately.

Tip Use jalapeño chillies if possible for this recipe as they have thicker flesh than many other chillies, making them easier to peel and stuff.

Serves 4-6 / **Preparation time** about 30 minutes / **Cooking time** 30 minutes

Serves 4 / **Preparation time** 20 minutes / **Cooking time** 8–10 minutes

deep-fried
corn cakes
tod mun khow phode

- **500 g (1 lb) corn cobs**
- **500 g (1 lb) minced pork (not too lean)**
- **1 tablespoon Garlic Mixture (see page 78)**
- **2 eggs, beaten**
- **2 tablespoons plain flour**
- **1 tablespoon cornflour**
- **1 teaspoon salt**
- **2 tablespoons light soy sauce**
- **½ vegetable stock cube, crumbled (optional)**
- **2 tablespoons coriander leaves, chopped, to garnish**
- **oil, for deep-frying**

TO SERVE

- **1 large cucumber, very finely sliced**
- **2 red chillies, deseeded and sliced into thin strips**

1 Working over a mixing bowl, slice all the kernels off the corn cobs with a sharp knife. Add the pork and garlic mixture and mix well, then stir in half of the beaten egg.

2 Add the plain flour, cornflour, salt and soy sauce, stirring well to make a mixture which is firm enough to be shaped. If necessary, add more beaten egg. Break off a small piece of the mixture and test-fry it in a little oil. If it tastes too bland, mix in half of the vegetable stock cube.

3 Form the mixture into round flat cakes, each about 4 cm (1½ inches) across. Heat the oil in a wok to 180–190°C (350–375°F), or until a cube of bread browns in 30 seconds, and deep-fry the corncakes, a few at a time, until golden brown. Drain on kitchen paper and leave to cool.

4 When cool, arrange the corn cakes on a serving plate and garnish with chopped coriander. Serve with cucumber slices and red chilli strips.

tow jio lon

vegetables with coconut and yellow bean sauce

- **about 500 g (1 lb) vegetables of your choice**
- **1 large fresh red chilli, sliced lengthways, to garnish**

COCONUT AND YELLOW BEAN SAUCE
- **125 ml (4 fl oz) yellow bean sauce**
- **½ onion, chopped**
- **1 tablespoon tamarind water**
- **250 ml (8 fl oz) coconut milk**
- **250 ml (8 fl oz) water**
- **2 eggs**
- **3 tablespoons sugar**
- **1 tablespoon soy sauce**

1 Choose a mixture of raw vegetables and chop them into bite-sized pieces.

2 To make the sauce, blend the yellow bean sauce and the onion in a food processor or blender and transfer to a saucepan. Add the rest of the sauce ingredients and bring gradually to the boil, stirring. Remove from the heat and pour into a bowl.

3 Garnish the sauce with the sliced chilli and serve warm, with the vegetables.

Tip Good vegetables for this dish are peeled broccoli stalks, carrot, cucumber and courgette sticks, thin green beans, Chinese leaves or cabbage, cauliflower florets and strips of red and yellow pepper

Serves 4 / **Preparation time** 15 minutes / **Cooking time** 5–6 minutes

bigger

bites

vegetable balls

thai fried pies

chicken dumplings

aubergine with shrimp paste sauce

thai egg strips

fried pork balls

spring rolls

hard-boiled eggs, thai-style

vegetables and seafood in batter

chicken satay

northern thai dip

mushroom and tofu satay

vegetable spring rolls

egg nets with pork and prawn filling

pork satay

chicken on lemon grass skewers

vegetable balls

pak chup ben tod

- ½ large onion, chopped
- 4 baby corn cobs, chopped
- 3 tablespoons carrot, grated
- 3 dried shiitake mushrooms, soaked, drained and sliced
- 25 g (1 oz) dried seaweed, soaked and drained
- 1 egg
- 1 teaspoon black pepper
- ½ teaspoon salt
- 4 garlic cloves, halved
- 150 g (5 oz) mashed potato
- 15 g (½ oz) fresh coriander
- 5 cm (2 inch) lemon grass stalk, thinly sliced
- 2 tablespoons cornflour mixed with 50 ml (2 fl oz) water
- groundnut oil, for deep-frying
- Plum Sauce (see page 77), to serve

1 Put the vegetables and seaweed in a food processor or blender and add the egg, pepper, salt, garlic, mashed potato, coriander and lemon grass. Blend to a smooth paste.

2 Spoon the paste into a saucepan and cook over a gentle heat, turning and stirring constantly, for 3 minutes. If the mixture is too loose, add a little of the cornflour mixture. Continue to stir and cook, adding more cornflour and water if necessary. When the mixture is the right consistency, form it into walnut-sized balls and chill in the refrigerator for 15 minutes.

3 Heat the oil for deep-frying in a wok. Drop in a few of the vegetable balls and deep-fry for 2–3 minutes, or until golden brown. Remove from the oil with a slotted spoon and drain on kitchen paper. Repeat with the remaining vegetable balls. Serve hot, with the plum sauce in a separate bowl.

Serves 4 / **Preparation time** 30 minutes, + soaking / **Cooking time** about 10 minutes

thai fried pies

pie thai tod

- **275 g (9 oz) plain flour**
- **¼ teaspoon salt**
- **125 g (4 oz) margarine**
- **2 tablespoons cold water**
- **groundnut oil, for deep-frying**
- **Hot Sweet Sauce (see page 76), to serve**

FILLING

- **500 g (1 lb) pumpkin, peeled and cut into chunks**
- **250 ml (8 fl oz) coconut milk**
- **1 tablespoon nam pla (fish sauce) or soy sauce**
- **1 lemon grass stalk, thinly sliced**
- **1 kaffir lime leaf, torn**
- **1 teaspoon crushed dried chillies**
- **1 teaspoon Red Curry Paste (see page 78)**
- **½ red pepper, cored, deseeded and diced**
- **½ onion, finely chopped**
- **3 tablespoons cooked carrot, finely diced**
- **3 tablespoons canned water chestnuts, finely diced**

1 First make the filling. Put the pumpkin, coconut milk, nam pla, lemon grass, lime leaf and chillies into a saucepan. Bring to the boil then simmer for about 15 minutes, until the pumpkin is tender. Mash the mixture in the pan; it should be quite thick. Remove from the heat and leave to cool.

2 Meanwhile, make the pastry. Sift the flour and salt into a bowl. Cut the fat into small pieces and rub in with the fingertips until the mixture resembles fine breadcrumbs. Add enough cold water to mix to a dough. Turn out the dough on a lightly floured surface and knead briefly. Cover and chill in the refrigerator for 10–15 minutes.

3 Add the curry paste, red pepper, onion, carrot and water chestnuts to the cold filling and mix together. Roll out the chilled dough thinly, and cut it into sixteen 7 cm (3 inch) circles.

4 Divide the filling among the dough circles, fold them in half and seal with a fork. Heat the oil for deep-frying in a wok, drop in half of the pies, and cook them over a moderate heat for 5–6 minutes until golden. Remove with a slotted spoon and drain on kitchen paper. Repeat with the remaining pies.

5 Serve hot or warm, with the sauce in a separate bowl.

Makes 16 / **Preparation time** about 40 minutes, + chilling / **Cooking time** about 10-12 minutes

Serves 4 / **Preparation time** 20-25 minutes / **Cooking time** 25-30 minutes

chicken dumplings

kha nom jeeb sai gai

- 3 tablespoons glutinous rice flour
- 250 g (9 oz) rice flour, plus 2 tablespoons
- 3 tablespoons arrowroot
- 350 ml (12 fl oz) water
- 2½ tablespoons vegetable oil
- banana leaves, for steaming (see below)

FILLING

- 4 tablespoons vegetable oil
- 2 tablespoons Garlic Mixture (see page 78)
- 500 g (1 lb) minced chicken
- 1 onion, finely chopped
- 3 tablespoons nam pla (fish sauce)
- 3 tablespoons sugar

TO SERVE

- 1-2 tablespoons Garlic Oil (see page 76)
- 1 lettuce, separated into leaves
- ½ cucumber, sliced
- 1 bunch of spring onions, sliced

Tip If you can't find any banana leaves in your local markets, use a sheet of foil instead. It serves the same purpose but of course it does not give any flavour to the chicken dumplings.

1 First prepare the dough. Place the rice flour in a heavy-based saucepan with 250 g (9 oz) of the rice flour and 1 tablespoon of the arrowroot. Stir in the water and oil.

2 Place the pan over a moderate heat and cook, stirring constantly, until the mixture forms a ball, leaving the sides of the pan clean. Transfer the mixture to a bowl and leave to cool slightly. When the dough is still just warm, add the remaining rice flour and arrowroot and knead until smooth and shiny. Cover the bowl with a damp cloth and set aside while preparing the filling.

3 Heat 2 tablespoons of the oil in a frying pan, add the garlic mixture and stir-fry for 1 minute. Add the chicken and stir-fry for 3–5 minutes. Stir in the onion, nam pla and sugar and cook, stirring, until all the liquid has been absorbed. Spoon into a bowl and set aside until cold.

4 Roll the dough into small balls, about 1 cm (½ inch) in diameter, then flatten each ball to a round. Place a heaped teaspoon of the filling in the centre of each one. Crimp the edges.

5 Put a layer of torn banana leaves in the top of a steamer. Brush the leaves with the remaining oil and prick them all over with a fork. Arrange the dumplings on top of the banana leaves. Steam for 10–15 minutes until cooked. To serve, brush the dumplings generously with garlic oil and arrange on a large platter. Serve with a lettuce, cucumber and spring onion salad.

aubergine with shrimp paste sauce

nam prig bhug

- **3 small garlic cloves, chopped**
- **4–5 small fresh red chillies, chopped**
- **1 tablespoon shrimp paste**
- **2 tablespoons lemon juice**
- **1 tablespoon brown sugar**
- **½ teaspoon nam pla (fish sauce)**
- **1 teaspoon ground dried shrimp**
- **3 aubergines**
- **1 egg, beaten**
- **oil, for deep-frying**

1 First make the shrimp paste sauce. Put the chopped garlic and red chillies into a mortar and then grind them until they are well blended and form a thick paste. Transfer the garlic and chilli mixture to a small bowl and add the shrimp paste, lemon juice, sugar, nam pla and ground dried shrimp. Mix together until they are thoroughly combined. Set aside while you cook the aubergines.

2 Cut the aubergines into thick slices. Put the beaten egg into a shallow bowl and coat the aubergine thoroughly.

3 Heat the oil for deep-frying in a wok and fry the aubergine slices in batches until they are golden brown, turning them once. Remove with a slotted spoon and drain on kitchen paper. Serve hot with the shrimp paste sauce.

Serves 4 / **Preparation time** 15 minutes / **Cooking time** 5-10 minutes

thai egg strips

kai tiaow

- **3 eggs, beaten**
- **1 shallot, finely sliced**
- **green shoots of 1 spring onion, sliced**
- **1–2 small red chillies, finely chopped**
- **1 tablespoon coriander leaves, chopped**
- **1 tablespoon groundnut oil**
- **salt and pepper**
- **julienne strips of spring onions, to garnish (optional)**

1 Mix all the ingredients, except the oil, in a bowl. Season to taste with salt and pepper.

2 Heat the oil in a wok, pour in the egg mixture and swirl it around the pan to produce a large thin omelette. Cook for 1–2 minutes until firm. Slide the omelette out on to a plate and roll it up like a pancake. Leave to cool.

3 When the omelette roll is cool, cut it crossways into 5 mm (¼ inch) or 1 cm (½ inch) sections, depending on how wide you want your strips to be. Serve them rolled up or straightened out, in a heap. Garnish with strips of spring onion, if wished.

Serves 2 / **Preparation time** 5 minutes, + cooling / **Cooking time** 2-3 minutes

Serves 4 / **Preparation time** 15 minutes / **Cooking time** 12 minutes

fried pork balls
moo tod

1 Put the coriander stems, pepper, garlic and sugar into a mortar or blender and work to a smooth paste.

2 Put the pork and the coriander paste into a food processor or blender and add the nam pla. Process until the mixture is thick and smooth, then transfer to a bowl.

3 Form the mixture into about 20 small balls, about 2.5 cm (1 inch) in diameter. Roll the pork balls lightly in a little flour.

4 Heat the oil in a wok, add about 5 pork balls and fry over a moderate heat for 2–3 minutes, or until no liquid is released from the pork balls when they are pierced with a knife. Remove from the wok with a slotted spoon and drain on kitchen paper. Keep warm while you fry the remaining pork balls. Serve hot garnished with coriander leaves.

- **2 teaspoons coriander stems, chopped**
- **2 teaspoons black pepper**
- **4 garlic cloves, peeled**
- **pinch of sugar**
- **500 g (1 lb) minced pork**
- **2 tablespoons nam pla (fish sauce)**
- **flour, for coating**
- **4–5 tablespoons vegetable oil**
- **coriander leaves, to garnish**

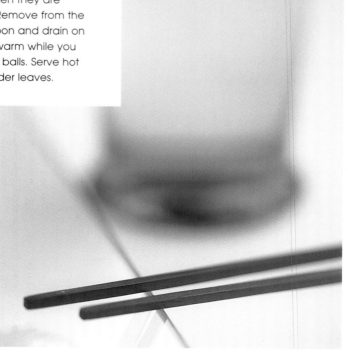

spring rolls

poh piah tod

- **250 g (8 oz) spring roll wrappers, each 12 cm (5 inches) square**
- **1 egg, beaten**
- **oil, for deep-frying**

FILLING

- **2 tablespoons vegetable oil**
- **2 tablespoons Garlic Mixture (see page 78)**
- **125 g (4 oz) crab meat**
- **125 g (4 oz) raw prawns, shelled and finely chopped**
- **125 g (4 oz) minced pork**
- **125 g (4 oz) vermicelli, soaked and cut into 1 cm (½ inch) lengths**
- **125 g (4 oz) mushrooms, chopped**
- **2 tablespoons nam pla (fish sauce)**
- **2 tablespoons light soy sauce**
- **1 teaspoon sugar**
- **5 spring onions, finely chopped**

TO GARNISH

- **1 large red chilli, cut into fine julienne strips**
- **1 lime, sliced**
- **basil leaves**

1. First make the filling. Heat the oil in a wok, add the garlic mixture and stir-fry for 1 minute until golden brown. Add the crab meat, prawns and pork and stir-fry for 10–12 minutes, or until lightly cooked. Add the vermicelli, mushrooms, nam pla, soy sauce, sugar and spring onions, and stir-fry for a further 5 minutes until all the liquid has been absorbed. Set aside to cool.

2. Separate the spring roll wrappers and arrange them on a work surface. Cover with a clean tea towel to keep them soft. Put about 2 tablespoons of the filling on each wrapper, and brush the left and right edges with beaten egg. Fold the sides over the filling then roll up the wrappers like a sausage. Brush the top edge with more beaten egg and then seal. Keep the filled rolls covered while you make the remaining spring rolls in the same way.

3. Heat the oil in a wok and cook the spring rolls, a few at a time, for 5–8 minutes, or until golden brown. Turn them once during cooking so that they brown evenly. Drain on kitchen paper and serve hot, garnished with strips of red chilli, slices of lime and a few basil leaves.

Serves 6 / **Preparation time** 25 minutes / **Cooking time** 20-25 minutes

hard-boiled eggs, thai-style

khai loog kheoy

- 1 teaspoon vinegar
- 6 eggs
- 4½ tablespoons vegetable oil
- 1 tablespoon dried red chillies
- 4 shallots, finely chopped
- 125 ml (4 fl oz) Tamarind Sauce (see page 78)
- 2 teaspoons dark soy sauce

1 Bring a saucepan of water to the boil. Stir in the vinegar, then lower the heat and carefully add the eggs. Boil gently for 6–7 minutes, then drain and run the eggs under cold water until cool. Shell them carefully and set aside.

2 Heat ½ tablespoon of the oil in a small frying pan. Add the dried red chillies and fry until they are crisp. Drain on kitchen paper and set aside.

3 Heat the remaining oil in a wok. Add the eggs and fry, turning constantly with a wooden spoon, until golden brown. Remove each egg as it browns and drain on kitchen paper.

4 Add the shallots to the wok and fry quickly until golden brown. Transfer to a small dish and keep warm. Pour away all but 2 tablespoons of oil from the wok. Add the tamarind sauce and soy sauce and boil until the mixture thickens. Meanwhile, quarter the eggs lengthways and arrange on a serving dish. Pour the tamarind sauce over the top and sprinkle with the fried shallots and chillies.

Serves 4-6 / **Preparation time** 15 minutes / **Cooking time** 15 minutes

vegetables and seafood in batter

gung pla choob pang tod

- **1 teaspoon Garlic Mixture (see page 78)**
- **1 teaspoon nam pla (fish sauce)**
- **125 g (4 oz) mixed fish or shellfish (see below)**
- **oil, for deep-frying**
- **8 string beans**
- **1 green pepper, cored, deseeded and cut into 8 pieces**
- **1 large carrot, quartered lengthways**
- **4 baby corn cobs**
- **Plum Sauce (see page 77), to serve**

TEMPURA BATTER

- **1 egg**
- **150 ml (½ pint) cold water**
- **125 g (4 oz) self-raising flour**
- **2 tablespoons cornflour**
- **1 teaspoon baking powder**

1 Combine the garlic mixture, nam pla and fish or shellfish in a shallow dish. Set aside for 5 minutes.

2 To make the tempura batter, mix the egg and water in a bowl. Sift in the flour, cornflour and baking powder and mix in quickly with a fork or a pair of chop-sticks. Do not overmix, the batter should still be slightly lumpy.

3 Heat the oil in a wok or deep-fat fryer. Dip the vegetables, one by one, into the batter and deep-fry until puffed and golden. Drain on kitchen paper. Cook the fish or shellfish in the same way. Do not cook too much at once, or the temperature of the oil will fall and the results will be unsatisfactory.

4 Transfer the cooked fish and vegetables to a warmed serving platter and serve immediately, with a bowl of plum sauce.

Tip Any kind of firm fish or shellfish may be used for this recipe. Filleted fish should be cut into 1 cm (½ inch) thick slices; squid should be cleaned and cut into 1 cm (½ inch) rings and crab claws should be shelled.

Serves 4 / **Preparation time** 10 minutes / **Cooking time** 20 minutes

chicken satay

sate gai

- **500 g (1 lb) chicken breast, thinly sliced into 5 x 2.5 cm (2 x 1 inch) slices**
- **Easy Satay Sauce (see page 79)**

MARINADE

- **1 tablespoon ground cinnamon**
- **1 tablespoon ground cumin**
- **1 teaspoon black pepper**
- **150 ml (¼ pint) oil**
- **100 ml (3½ fl oz) light soy sauce**
- **2 tablespoons palm sugar or light muscovado sugar**

TO GARNISH

- **raw onion, roughly chopped**
- **cucumber chunks**

1 Put the chicken slices into a container and add all the marinade ingredients. Stir very thoroughly and make sure that all the chicken pieces are coated in the marinade. Leave for at least 4 hours, or preferably overnight. Give it an occasional stir.

2 Carefully thread the chicken pieces on to 8–12 bamboo skewers, leaving some space at either end. Place them under a preheated hot grill for about 2 minutes, turning once. As you cannot see if the chicken is cooked through, test one piece – you can always grill it for a little longer if necessary. You will have to cook the skewers in batches, so keep the cooked chicken warm while waiting for the rest to be done.

3 Garnish the skewers with chopped raw onion and cucumber chunks and serve with the satay sauce.

Serves 4 / **Preparation time** 10-15 minutes, + marinating / **Cooking time** 10 minutes

northern thai dip
nam prik ong

- **1 teaspoon shrimp paste (optional)**
- **4 shallots, finely chopped**
- **6 red bird chillies, finely chopped**
- **2 coriander roots, finely chopped**
- **4 garlic cloves, crushed**
- **2 tablespoons vegetable oil**
- **500 g (1 lb) minced pork**
- **2 firm tomatoes, finely chopped**
- **1 teaspoon brown sugar**
- **4 spring onions, finely sliced**
- **1 tablespoon nam pla (fish sauce)**
- **2 tablespoons chicken stock**
- **handful of coriander leaves, chopped**
- **selection of raw vegetables, to serve**

1 Put the shrimp paste, if using, shallots, chillies, coriander roots and garlic into a mortar or food processor and blend to make a paste. Heat the oil in a frying pan until hot and fry the paste for 2–3 minutes to cook the shallots.

2 With the frying pan still searing hot, add the pork to the pan and stir-fry for 5–6 minutes or until the pork is cooked through. Add the tomatoes, sugar, spring onions, nam pla and chicken stock and simmer for a further 5 minutes.

3 Leave the dip to cool slightly then mix in the chopped coriander. Serve with a selection of raw vegetables.

Information
In Thailand, this aromatic and fiery-hot dip is served with exotic vegetables, such as round white or yellow aubergines, yard beans, steamed banana flowers, boiled bamboo shoots and assorted lettuce leaves. Failing any of these, it is equally good with chicory leaves, small sweet Cos lettuce leaves and cherry tomatoes.

Serves 4-6 / **Preparation time** 10 minutes / **Cooking time** 14-16 minutes

mushroom and tofu satay

sate het tahu

- **2 x 250 g (8 oz) blocks ready-fried tofu, sliced**
- **200 g (7 oz) fresh shiitake or exotic mushrooms**
- **8–12 satay sticks**

MARINADE

- **125 ml (4 fl oz) dark soy sauce**
- **50 ml (2 fl oz) water**
- **1 tablespoon palm sugar or soft brown sugar**
- **2 garlic cloves, chopped**

TO SERVE

- **cucumber chunks**
- **spring onions, finely sliced lengthways**
- **Easy Satay Sauce (see page 79)**

1 Cut the sliced tofu into 3 cm (1½ inch) lengths. Cut any large mushrooms in half. Put the marinade ingredients into a shallow bowl, add the tofu and mushrooms and stir around to coat them on all sides. Cover and leave to marinate for 1 hour.

2 Remove the satay sticks from the water (see Tip, below), one at a time, and carefully thread the tofu and mushrooms on them. Cook under a preheated hot grill for 1–2 minutes on each side. Serve hot, garnished with cucumber chunks and sliced spring onions, with the sauce in a separate bowl.

Tip To cook these satay sticks, you will need 8–12 wooden or bamboo skewers. Soak them in cold water for 20–30 minutes before you use them, to prevent them burning.

Makes 8–12 / **Preparation time** 10 minutes, + marinating / **Cooking time** 10 minutes

vegetable spring rolls
bapia tod

- **12 square spring roll wrappers**
- **groundnut oil, for deep-frying**
- **coriander leaves, to garnish**

FILLING

- **1 tablespoon groundnut oil**
- **2 garlic cloves, finely chopped**
- **40 g (1½ oz) bean sprouts**
- **50 g (2 oz) shredded white cabbage**
- **2 fresh shiitake mushrooms, sliced**
- **2 tablespoons celery leaves and stalks, finely chopped**
- **1 teaspoon sugar**
- **2 teaspoons soy sauce**
- **50 g (2 oz) dried bean thread noodles, soaked, drained and cut into short lengths with scissors**
- **Soy and Vinegar Dipping Sauce (see page 76), to serve**

1 First make the filling. Heat a wok, add the oil, garlic, bean sprouts, cabbage, mushrooms and celery and stir-fry for 30 seconds. Add the sugar, soy sauce and noodles and stir-fry for 1 minute, then remove from the heat and transfer the vegetables on to a plate. Wipe the wok clean with kitchen paper.

2 Put 1 tablespoon of the filling on one corner of a spring roll wrapper and roll it up, folding in the ends to form a neat tube. Use a little oil to stick down the last corner, then secure the roll with a cocktail stick. Repeat with the remaining wrappers and filling.

3 Heat the oil in a wok, add a batch of spring rolls, and cook over a moderate heat for 3–4 minutes until golden brown on all sides. Remove from the oil with a slotted spoon and drain on kitchen paper. Repeat with the remaining spring rolls.

4 Remove the cocktail sticks. Serve hot, with dipping sauce in a separate bowl and garnished with coriander leaves.

Makes 12 / **Preparation time** 15-20 minutes, + soaking / **Cooking time** 3-4 minutes per batch

egg nets with pork & prawn filling *lhrum*

- **6 eggs, lightly beaten**
- **2 red chillies, deseeded and sliced into thin strips**
- **4 tablespoons torn coriander leaves**
- **Chilli Sauce (see page 76), to serve**

FILLING
- **3 tablespoons vegetable oil**
- **1 tablespoon Garlic Mixture (see page 78)**
- **250 g (8 oz) minced pork**
- **125 g (4 oz) raw prawns, peeled, deveined and minced**
- **2 tablespoons chopped onion, finely chopped**
- **3 tablespoons nam pla (fish sauce)**
- **3 tablespoons sugar**
- **125 g (4 oz) crushed roasted peanuts (see page 77)**

TO GARNISH
- **½ red pepper, cored, deseeded and thinly sliced**
- **½ green pepper, cored, deseeded and thinly sliced**

1 First prepare the filling. Heat 2 table-spoons of the oil in a wok, add the garlic mixture and stir-fry for 1 minute. Add the pork and stir-fry for 5–7 minutes, then add the remaining ingredients except the peanuts and cook, stirring, for 3 minutes. Remove the pan from the heat, stir in the peanuts and set aside.

2 Brush a wok with some of the remaining oil and place it over a moderate heat. Fit a 5 mm (¼ inch) nozzle into a piping bag and spoon a little of the beaten egg mixture into the bag, keeping the nozzle stopped with a finger. Holding the bag over the wok, remove your fin-ger and drizzle the egg into the centre of the wok in a flat square lattice, meas-uring about 9 cm (3½ inches) square. As soon as the egg lattice is cooked, slide it on to a plate and keep it warm. Continue to make egg lattices until all the egg mixture has been used, brush-ing the wok with more oil as necessary.

3 To make the nets, make a cross from 2 pieces of chilli in the centre of each egg lattice square. Place a coriander leaf on top of the chilli and add a heaped tea-spoon of the prepared filling. Carefully fold the egg lattice over the filling to form a parcel shape. Repeat with the remaining lattice shapes and filling. Arrange the nets on a serving platter in such a way that the red of the chilli and the green of the coriander can clearly be seen. Serve immediately, garnished with red and green pepper strips, and with a bowl of chilli sauce.

Serves 4 / **Preparation time** 10 minutes
Cooking time 20 minutes

pork satay

sate bhud

- **500 g (1 lb) pork fillet**
- **2 teaspoons palm sugar or soft brown sugar**
- **1 teaspoon salt**
- **1 teaspoon turmeric**
- **1 teaspoon ground coriander**
- **1 teaspoon ground cumin**
- **175 ml (6 fl oz) coconut milk**
- **chilli powder, for sprinkling**
- **coriander sprigs, to garnish**
- **lemon slices, to serve**

PEANUT SAUCE
- **50 g (2 oz) peanuts, roasted**
- **1 teaspoon salt**
- **300 ml (½ pint) coconut milk**
- **2 teaspoons Red Curry Paste (see page 78)**
- **2 tablespoons sugar**
- **½ teaspoon lemon juice**

1 Cut the pork into 5 cm (2 inch) strips and put them into a large bowl. Add the sugar, salt, turmeric, coriander, cumin and 4 tablespoons of the coconut milk and knead the spices into the meat with your hands. Cover and leave to marinate for at least 2 hours.

2 To make the sauce, grind the peanuts with the salt in a mortar until the mixture turns to a thick cream. Set aside. Put half the coconut milk into a saucepan with the curry paste. Heat gently for 3 minutes, stirring constantly. Stir in the ground peanuts with the sugar, lemon juice and the remaining coconut milk. Simmer gently for 20–30 minutes, stirring often to prevent the sauce from sticking. Transfer to a bowl.

3 Thread the marinated pork on to oiled skewers and cook on a barbecue or under a preheated hot grill for 12–15 minutes, turning them several times and brushing frequently with the reserved coconut milk. Sprinkle the kebabs with chilli powder, garnish with sprigs of coriander and serve with the peanut sauce and some lemon slices.

Serves 4 / **Preparation time** 15-20 minutes, + marinating /
Cooking time 45 minutes

chicken on lemon grass skewers

gy young da kry

- **300 g (10 oz) minced chicken**
- **1 garlic clove, crushed**
- **1 teaspoon fresh root ginger, grated**
- **1 tablespoon nam pla (fish sauce)**
- **2 teaspoons ground cumin**
- **2 teaspoons ground coriander**
- **1 tablespoon coriander leaves, finely chopped**
- **1 red chilli, deseeded and finely chopped**
- **1 teaspoon sugar**
- **grated rind and juice of 1 lime**
- **1 tablespoon desiccated coconut**
- **8 lemon grass stalks**
- **salt and pepper**

1 Put all the ingredients except the lemon grass into a bowl. Season well, then use your hands to pound and press the mixture together until thoroughly blended. Cover and chill for 10 minutes.

2 When you are ready to cook the skewers, divide the chicken mixture into 8 equal-sized portions. Mould a portion of the spicy chicken mixture on to the end of a lemon grass stalk, forming a sausage shape. Repeat with the remaining portions of spicy chicken mixture and lemon grass stalks.

3 Heat the grill to the hottest setting and cook the skewers for 5–6 minutes on each side or until the chicken mixture is cooked through. Serve hot, with boiled rice and a mixed salad.

Tip This is a most imaginative and delicious way of cooking chicken kebabs. The flavour of the lemon grass stalks is released as they cook, infusing the chicken with a heady perfume and subtle spice

Serves 4 / **Preparation time** 10 minutes / **Cooking time** 10-12 minutes

a bite more

grilled chicken, sala thai style

pork with hot sauces

stuffed green peppers

beef and galangal salad

fish cakes with spicy dipping sauce

spare ribs

griddled prawn cakes

vegetable samosas

stuffed aubergines

hot thai beef salad

fresh fruit platter

grilled chicken, sala thai style

gai yang

- **8 chicken drumsticks**
- **2 tablespoons Garlic Mixture (see page 78)**
- **1 teaspoon salt**
- **2 tablespoons dark soy sauce**
- **3 tablespoons clear honey**
- **2 teaspoons ground ginger**
- **1 tablespoon oyster sauce**

Tip In Thailand, this chicken dish is traditionally served with steamed sticky or glutinous rice and a sweet and sour salad.

1 Place the chicken drumsticks on a board and pierce them all over with a fork.

2 Combine all the remaining ingredients in a shallow dish large enough to hold the drumsticks in a single layer. Add the drumsticks and turn to coat well. Cover and set aside to marinate for at least 2 hours.

3 Grill the marinated drumsticks on a barbecue over medium hot coals for 30 minutes, turning the chicken over halfway through, or cook under a preheated conventional grill. Serve immediately.

Serves 4 / **Preparation time** 10 minutes, + marinating / **Cooking time** 30 minutes

pork
with hot
sauces

moo thod katiem

- **375 g (12 oz) pork fillet**
- **½ teaspoon salt**
- **¼ teaspoon white pepper**
- **15 g (½ oz) butter**
- **1 tablespoon oil**
- **3 garlic cloves, finely chopped**
- **1 cm (½ inch) piece of fresh root ginger, chopped**
- **2 red chillies, chopped**
- **1½ teaspoons ground cumin**
- **½ cucumber, finely diced, to serve**

CHILLI AND GINGER SAUCE

- **2 red chillies, chopped**
- **2.5 cm (1 inch) piece of fresh root ginger, chopped**
- **½ onion, grated**
- **salt**

TOMATO AND CHILLI SAUCE

- **2 tomatoes, skinned and chopped**
- **2 garlic cloves, crushed**
- **pinch of sugar**
- **1 teaspoon hot chilli powder**
- **salt**

1   Slice the pork thinly and rub with salt and pepper. Heat the butter and oil in a wok over a moderate heat. Add the pork and stir-fry until lightly browned. Remove from the wok and keep warm.

2   Add the garlic to the wok with the ginger, chillies and cumin. Stir-fry for 2 minutes then return the pork to the wok. Stir-fry for 2 minutes over a low heat, or until the meat is tender. If necessary, add a sprinkling of water to keep the meat moist.

3   To make the chilli and ginger sauce, put the chillies, ginger, onion and salt in a mortar and pound until you have a smooth paste.

4   To make the tomato and chilli sauce, put the chopped tomatoes and garlic in a small bowl, and mix in a good pinch of sugar, the hot chilli powder and salt to taste. Serve the stir-fried pork with the diced cucumber and the two hot sauces.

Serves 4 / **Preparation time** 15 minutes / **Cooking time** 8-10 minutes

Makes 8 / **Preparation time** 20 minutes / **Cooking time** 15-20 minutes

stuffed green peppers

prik kiaow yat sai

- **8 large mild green peppers**
- **groundnut oil, for deep-frying**
- **whole chives, to garnish**

FILLING

- **3 baby corn cobs, roughly chopped**
- **3 garlic cloves, halved**
- **4 tablespoons groundnut oil**
- **½ large onion, finely chopped**
- **1 tomato, diced**
- **2 fresh shiitake or chestnut mushrooms, finely sliced**
- **50 g (2 oz) green beans, finely sliced**
- **½ teaspoon sugar**
- **1 tablespoon soy sauce**
- **¼ teaspoon salt**
- **1 teaspoon pepper**
- **2 eggs**

BATTER

- **3 tablespoons cornflour**
- **50 ml (2 fl oz) water**
- **½ teaspoon salt**
- **¼ teaspoon pepper**

1 Remove the ends from the green peppers and discard the seeds. Set the hollow peppers aside.

2 To make the filling, blend the corn and garlic in a food processor or blender. Heat 3 tablespoons of the oil in a wok and cook the onion for 30 seconds. Add the tomato and mushrooms and cook, stirring, for 1 minute. Add the green beans and cook for 30 seconds then add the corn and garlic mixture, the sugar, soy sauce and salt and pepper. At this point you may need to add the remaining oil. Break the eggs into the mixture and give them a good stir. Cook for 2 minutes, remove from the heat and turn the mixture out on to a plate. Stuff the peppers with the filling, as full as you can.

3 Put the batter ingredients into a bowl and mix thoroughly.

4 Heat the oil for deep-frying in a wok. Coat half of the peppers in the batter, pop them in the hot oil and cook for 6–7 minutes, moving them around gently until they are golden on all sides. Remove the peppers from the oil with a slotted spoon and drain on kitchen paper. Repeat with the remaining peppers and batter. Arrange the cooked peppers on a plate, garnish with chives and serve immediately.

Tip For this recipe use long green peppers rather than the squat bell-shaped variety. They should be about 20 cm (8 inches) long and 2–2.5 (½–1 inch) wide at their fattest part. If you can't find long peppers, use 4 bell-shaped ones instead. You can make the stuffing and fill the peppers in advance, then coat them in batter and deep-fry them at the last minute.

beef and galangal salad

larb nua

- **2 tablespoons glutinous rice**
- **300 g (10 oz) minced beef**
- **5 thin slices galangal or fresh root ginger**
- **3 tablespoons spring onion, finely chopped**
- **1 teaspoon chilli powder**
- **3–4 tablespoons lemon juice**
- **2 tablespoons nam pla (fish sauce)**
- **½ teaspoon sugar**
- **4–5 mint sprigs, leaves chopped**
- **3 tablespoons shallots, chopped**
- **1 crisp lettuce, separated into leaves, to serve**
- **mint sprigs, to garnish**

1 Place the glutinous rice in a saucepan over a moderate heat and dry-fry, stirring constantly, for 10 minutes, or until the grains turn light brown. Remove from the heat. Grind in a food processor or blender, or pound in a mortar until the rice is very fine.

2 Place the minced beef in a saucepan and cook over a gentle heat for 10–15 minutes, stirring constantly, until the meat is cooked and all the liquid has been absorbed. Transfer to a bowl and stir in the ground rice. Add the galangal or ginger, spring onions, chilli powder, lemon juice, nam pla, sugar, mint and shallots and mix well.

3 Arrange the lettuce on a shallow dish, and top with the beef mixture. Garnish with mint sprigs and serve at once.

Serves 4 / **Preparation time** 10 minutes / **Cooking time** 20-25 minutes

fish cakes with spicy dipping sauce

tod man plaa

- 3 red bird chillies, chopped
- 2 green bird chillies, chopped
- 2.5 cm (1 inch) piece of galangal, peeled and finely chopped
- 1 lemon grass stalk, finely chopped
- 2 coriander roots, chopped
- 2 tablespoons coriander leaves, chopped
- 2 kaffir lime leaves, shredded
- 3 garlic cloves, finely chopped
- 4 shallots, finely chopped
- 1 tablespoon nam pla (fish sauce)
- 1 teaspoon coriander seeds, crushed
- 500 g (1 lb) white fish fillets, such as cod, haddock or whiting, skinned and roughly chopped
- 1 small egg, beaten
- 2 teaspoons palm sugar or brown sugar
- oil, for deep-frying

SWEET AND SOUR CUCUMBER DIPPING SAUCE

- 125 ml (4 fl oz) rice vinegar
- 2 tablespoons caster sugar
- 2 tablespoons water
- 2 tablespoons nam pla (fish sauce)
- 2.5 cm (1 inch) piece cucumber, diced
- 1 shallot, roughly chopped
- 1 tablespoon carrot, grated
- 1 red bird chilli, sliced
- 1 green bird chilli, sliced

1 Put the red and green chillies, galangal, lemon grass, coriander roots and leaves. lime leaves, garlic, shallots, nam pla and coriander seeds into a food processor and blend to a smooth paste. Add the fish and blend to a rough paste. Add the egg and sugar and blend once more until smooth.

2 To make the dipping sauce, put the vinegar, sugar, water and nam pla in a small saucepan and heat until the sugar has dissolved. Remove from the heat, leave to cool then add the cucumber, shallot, carrot and chillies.

3 With damp hands, divide the fish mixture into walnut-sized balls and flatten them with the heel of your hand into small fish cakes. Heat the oil for deep-frying in a wok until a piece of bread browns in 2 minutes. Add a few fish cakes at a time to the hot oil and cook for 2–3 minutes or until golden brown, turning once.

4 Remove the fish cakes from the oil with a slotted spoon and drain on kitchen paper while frying the remainder. Serve with the dipping sauce.

Serves 4 / **Preparation time** 15-20 minutes / **Cooking time** 10-15 minutes

spare ribs *gat doog moo*

- **4 large or 8 small pork spare ribs, weighing about 475 g (15 oz) in total**

MARINADE

- **1½ tablespoons palm sugar or light muscovado sugar**
- **3 tablespoons light soy sauce**
- **1 tablespoon oyster sauce**
- **1 teaspoon ground black pepper**
- **6 large garlic cloves, chopped**

1 Mix together all the ingredients for the marinade in a bowl. Add the spare ribs, turning them thoroughly to coat them all over with the marinade. The longer you leave them the tastier they will be, but they will need at least 2 hours.

2 Place the spare ribs on a baking sheet, with as much of the marinade as possible, and cook in a preheated oven, 180°C (350°F), Gas Mark 4, for 40 minutes.

Serves 4 / **Preparation time** 2-3 minutes, + marinating / **Cooking time** 40 minutes

griddled prawn cakes

tod mun gung

- **500 g (1 lb) cooked peeled prawns**
- **1 garlic clove, crushed**
- **2.5 cm (1 inch) piece of fresh root ginger, diced**
- **2 red chillies, chopped**
- **1 bunch of coriander, chopped**
- **2 teaspoons nam pla (fish sauce)**
- **1 egg yolk**
- **250 g (8 oz) mashed potatoes**
- **soy or Chilli sauce (see page 76), to serve**

1 Place the prawns in a food processor or blender with the garlic, ginger, chillies, coriander, nam pla and egg yolk. Process until smooth.

2 Mix the prawn mixture thoroughly with the mashed potatoes, using a fork. Divide the mixture into 12 cakes (or about 24 smaller ones), dusting your hands in flour if the mixture is sticky.

3 Heat a griddle pan. Place the prawn cakes on the griddle and cook for 5 minutes on each side. Keep the batches warm while the remaining prawn cakes are being cooked.

4 Serve with some soy or chilli sauce.

Variation Substitute 500 g (1 lb) cooked fish, such as salmon, cod or haddock, for the prawns and continue as in the main recipe.

vegetable samosas

pak sa mo sa

- **16 square wonton wrappers**
- **a little cornflour and water paste, to seal**
- **groundnut oil, for deep-frying**

FILLING

- **250 g (8 oz) diced potato**
- **1 tablespoon groundnut oil**
- **2 tablespoons finely chopped shallot**
- **2 garlic cloves, finely chopped**
- **50 ml (2 fl oz) coconut milk**
- **2 heaped teaspoons Yellow Curry Paste (see page 78)**
- **75 g (3 oz) peas**
- **juice of ½ lime**
- **½ teaspoon salt or to taste**

TO SERVE

- **coriander leaves**
- **juice of 1 lime**

1   First make the filling. Boil the diced potato until tender then drain and set aside. Heat the oil in a small saucepan and cook the shallot and garlic until golden. Drain and set aside. In a saucepan, gently heat the coconut milk and curry paste, stirring until smooth, then add the potato, the shallot and garlic mixture, peas, lime juice and salt. Mash coarsely then remove from the heat and set aside.

2   Take 2 wonton wrappers together to make a double thickness, and put a spoonful of the potato mixture in the centre. Fold the wrappers over to make a triangle, then seal the edges with a little cornflour and water paste. Repeat with the remaining wrappers and filling.

3   Heat the oil for deep-frying in a wok, drop in half the samosas and cook over a moderate heat for 3–4 minutes, until golden brown on all sides. Remove from the oil with a slotted spoon and drain on kitchen paper. Repeat with the remaining samosas.

4   Arrange the samosas on a serving dish, sprinkle with coriander leaves and lime juice, and serve at once.

Makes 8 / **Preparation time** 30 minutes / **Cooking time** 3-4 minutes per batch

stuffed aubergines

kayanthi hnat

- **24 small Thai aubergines**
- **50 g (2 oz) raw prawns, peeled**
- **75 g (3 oz) boneless, skinless chicken breast**
- **1 spring onion, finely chopped**
- **4 garlic cloves, crushed**
- **1 tablespoon chilli powder**
- **1 teaspoon turmeric**
- **1 tablespoon chopped coriander or parsley**
- **2 tablespoons vegetable oil**
- **1 egg**
- **3 tablespoons cornflour**
- **2 tablespoons plain flour**
- **oil, for deep-frying**
- **salt**
- **Chilli Sauce (see page 76), to serve**

1 Wash the aubergines and pat dry. Cut off the tops and scoop out the centres. Cut the scooped-out flesh into small dice. Season with a little salt and set aside. Fill the empty shells with salted water and leave them to stand for 3–4 minutes then drain and rinse in fresh water.

2 Chop the prawns and chicken into small dice and place in a bowl. Add the spring onion, garlic and diced aubergine, and mix well. Season with chilli powder, turmeric and chopped coriander or parsley. Bind the ingredients together with the vegetable oil, and season with salt. Knead to a smooth paste and use this mixture to fill the aubergines.

3 Mix together the egg, cornflour and flour in a bowl, and add a little salt and cold water. Beat until you have a smooth, thick batter. Dip the filled aubergines into the batter so that they are thoroughly coated.

4 Heat the oil for deep-frying in a wok or deep-fryer, and fry the aubergines, a few at a time, until crisp and golden brown all over. Remove with a slotted spoon and drain on kitchen paper. Serve with chilli sauce.

Serves 4-6 / **Preparation time** 30 minutes / **Cooking time** 7-10 minutes

Serves 8 / **Preparation time** 15 minutes / **Cooking time** 5-10 minutes

hot thai
beef salad

yum nooer

- 2 tablespoons vegetable oil
- 500 g (1 lb) rump or fillet steak, cut across the grain into thin strips
- 2 garlic cloves, finely chopped
- 2 green chillies, finely sliced into rings
- juice of 2 lemons
- 1 tablespoon nam pla (fish sauce)
- 2 teaspoons caster sugar
- 2 ripe papayas, peeled and finely sliced
- ½ large cucumber, cut into matchstick strips
- 75 g (3 oz) bean sprouts
- 1 crisp lettuce, shredded
- Chilli Sauce (see page 76), to serve

1 Heat a wok, add the oil and place over a moderate heat until hot. Add the steak, garlic and chillies, increase the heat to high and stir-fry for 3–4 minutes or until the steak is browned on all sides. Pour in the lemon juice and nam pla, add the sugar and stir-fry until sizzling.

2 Remove the wok from the heat. Lift the steak out of the liquid with a slotted spoon and toss with the papayas, cucumber, bean sprouts and lettuce. Drizzle the liquid from the wok over the salad ingredients as a dressing and serve hot with a bowl of chilli sauce.

Tip This dish is sometimes served with the spicy meat on one side of the plate and the salad on the other, rather than mixed together.

fresh fruit platter

ponlamai zot

- **2 ripe mangoes**
- **1 small ripe papaya**
- **1 watermelon slice**
- **250 g (8 oz) lychees, peeled**
- **1 lime, cut into quarters**

1 Peel and thickly slice the mangoes and papaya into 4 or 8 pieces. Cut the watermelon into chunks, removing as many of the seeds as you can.

2 Arrange all of the fruit on a serving plate, and squeeze some lime juice over the papaya.

4)

little
meals

egg-fried noodles

thai-style coconut mussels

crisp fried fish with chilli and basil

braised chive flowers with prawns

barbecued chicken

chicken with burnt chilli paste and cashew nuts

crab omelette

green papaya salad

stir-fried squid with basil

vegetable stuffed omelette

yellow rice with mushrooms

shiitake, bamboo shoot and mangetout stir-fry

hot and sour noodle salad

egg-fried noodles

gung ob moh din

- **4 tablespoons groundnut oil**
- **1 garlic clove, crushed**
- **1 shallot or small onion, thinly sliced**
- **125 g (4 oz) fresh egg noodles**
- **grated rind of 1 lime**
- **2 teaspoons soy sauce**
- **2 tablespoons lime juice**
- **125 g (4 oz) chicken breast or pork fillet, sliced**
- **125 g (4 oz) crab meat or prepared squid**
- **125 g (4 oz) raw prawns, shelled**
- **1 tablespoon yellow soya bean paste**
- **1 tablespoon nam pla (fish sauce)**
- **2 tablespoons palm sugar or soft brown sugar**
- **2 eggs**
- **2 red chillies, deseeded and chopped**
- **pepper**

TO GARNISH

- **coriander leaves**
- **lime rind, finely sliced**

1 Heat half of the oil in a wok. Add the garlic and shallot and stir-fry quickly until golden and tender.

2 Plunge the egg noodles into boiling water for a few seconds. Drain well and then add to the wok. Stir-fry with the grated lime rind, soy sauce and lime juice for 3–4 minutes. Remove, drain and keep warm.

3 Add the remaining oil to the wok together with the chicken or pork, crab meat or squid and the prawns. Stir-fry over a high heat until cooked. Season with pepper, and stir in the soya bean paste, nam pla and sugar.

4 Break the eggs into the wok and stir gently until the mixture sets. Add the chillies and check the seasoning. Mix in the noodles and heat through over a low heat. Serve garnished with coriander leaves and lime rind.

Serves 8 / **Preparation time** 10 minutes / **Cooking time** 20 minutes

thai-style coconut mussels

gung ob

- **2 kg (4 lb) mussels**
- **600 ml (1 pint) vegetable stock**
- **400 ml (14 fl oz) coconut milk**
- **grated rind and juice of 2 limes**
- **2 lemon grass stalks, lightly bruised**
- **1 tablespoon Green Curry Paste (see page 77)**
- **3 red chillies, deseeded and finely sliced**
- **4 tablespoons chopped coriander leaves**
- **2 spring onions, shredded**
- **salt and pepper**

TO GARNISH (optional)

- **1 red chilli, deseeded and chopped**
- **coriander leaves, chopped**

1 Scrub the mussels in cold water, scrape off any barnacles and pull away the dark hairy beards that protrude from the shells. Discard any broken shells or open mussels that do not close when tapped sharply.

2 Pour the stock and coconut milk into a large saucepan and bring to the boil. Stir in the lime rind and juice, lemon grass, curry paste, chillies, coriander, spring onions and salt and pepper to taste. Add the mussels, cover the pan and bring back to the boil. Cook for 3–4 minutes or until all the mussels have opened. Discard any shells that remain closed. Use a slotted spoon to divide the mussels among 4 individual serving bowls and keep warm until ready to serve.

3 Bring the stock to a vigorous boil and boil hard for about 5 minutes to reduce it and concentrate the flavour. Strain the stock through a fine sieve, then ladle it over the mussels. Garnish the bowls of mussels with chopped red chilli and plenty of chopped coriander leaves. Serve immediately while still hot.

Serves 4 / **Preparation time** 10 minutes / **Cooking time** 20-25 minutes

crisp fried fish with chilli and basil

pla phad pet kaprow

- **3 garlic cloves, thinly sliced**
- **2 coriander roots, finely chopped**
- **2 fresh red chillies, finely chopped**
- **1 dried red chilli, finely chopped**
- **3 tablespoons caster sugar**
- **1 tablespoon groundnut oil**
- **3 tablespoons nam pla (fish sauce)**
- **3 tablespoons soy sauce**
- **3 lime leaves, finely shredded**
- **5 tablespoons fish stock or water**
- **oil, for deep-frying**
- **500 g (1 lb) catfish, sea bass or cod, filleted and cubed**

TO SERVE

- **20–30 holy basil leaves**
- **1 red chilli, shredded**

1 Blend the garlic, coriander roots, fresh and dried chillies and sugar in a food processor or pound to a paste in a mortar.

2 Heat 1 tablespoon of oil in a wok and stir-fry the chilli paste sauce for about 1–2 minutes. Add the nam pla, soy sauce and lime leaves and stir-fry for 1 minute then add the stock and bring to a fast boil. Continue to boil until the sauce has reduced.

3 Heat the oil for deep-frying in a saucepan and when it is hot add the pieces of fish and fry until crisp and golden brown. Remove the fish from the oil with a slotted spoon and add to the chilli paste sauce and toss together. Deep-fry the basil leaves for 30 seconds, remove and drain on kitchen paper.

4 Serve the fish topped with the deep-fried basil leaves and shreds of red chilli.

Tip Catfish is a dense and firm-fleshed fish, which stands up to deep-frying and plenty of chilli. They can be bought frozen in Thai stores and supermarkets in this country. Chop off the head and remove the fillets from the bone. Alternatively use sea bass or cod.

braised chive flowers with prawns

phat phak gau choy yaang

- **1 tablespoon groundnut oil**
- **2 garlic cloves, crushed**
- **175 g (6 oz) flowering chives, large chives or spring onions, cut into 7 cm (3 inch) lengths**
- **1 tablespoon nam pla (fish sauce)**
- **3 tablespoons dark soy sauce**
- **2 tablespoons caster sugar**
- **250 g (8 oz) small raw prawns, peeled and roughly chopped**
- **red chillies, sliced, to garnish**

1 Heat the oil in a wok, add the garlic and stir-fry for 1 minute. Add the chives or spring onions, nam pla, soy sauce and sugar and stir-fry for 1 further minute.

2 Add the raw prawns to the wok and stir-fry for 3 minutes until pink and cooked through. Serve immediately, garnished with red chillies. Thai jasmine rice makes a good accompaniment.

Tip Flowering chives (gau choy) are eaten all over South-east Asia, from China to Malaysia. They are used in China for flavouring dim sum and are also stir-fried as a vegetable. They have a strong garlic aroma and are best when very fresh. Keep them, wrapped, in the bottom of the refrigerator for up to 2 days.

barbecued chicken

gai yaang

- **1.5 kg (3 lb) chicken, spatchcocked, or part-boned chicken breasts**
- **5 cm (2 inch) piece of fresh galangal, peeled and finely chopped**
- **4 garlic cloves, crushed**
- **1 large red chilli, finely chopped**
- **4 shallots, finely chopped**
- **2 tablespoons finely chopped coriander leaves**
- **150 ml (¼ pint) thick coconut milk**
- **salt and pepper**
- **chive flowers, to garnish**

TO SERVE

- **1 quantity Chilli Sauce (see page 76)**
- **Sticky Rice (see page 79)**
- **lime wedges**

1 Rub the chicken all over with salt and pepper and place it in a shallow container.

2 Put the galangal, garlic, chilli, shallots and coriander in a food processor and blend to a paste. Add the coconut milk and mix until well blended. Pour the marinade over the chicken, cover and leave to marinate overnight in the refrigerator.

3 Remove the chicken from the marinade, place it on a hot barbecue and cook for 30–40 minutes for spatchcocked chicken and 10–15 minutes for the chicken breasts, turning and basting regularly with the remaining marinade. The whole chicken is cooked when a skewer inserted in one of the legs reveals clear juices.

4 Leave the chicken to stand for 5 minutes then chop it into small pieces with a cleaver. Serve with the dipping sauce, sticky rice and lime wedges. Garnish with chive flowers and eat with fingers.

Tip In Thailand this spatchcocked chicken is cooked gently over charcoal until tender and crisp, and served with a dipping sauce and sticky rice. Chicken portions can be used instead of a whole chicken, but only cook them for 10–15 minutes.

Serves 4-6 / **Preparation time** 20 minutes, + marinating /
Cooking time 10-15 or 30-40 minutes

chicken with burnt chilli paste and cashew nuts

gai nam prik pow
met ma muang

- 3 tablespoons groundnut oil or vegetable oil
- 2 garlic cloves, thinly sliced
- 375 g (12 oz) chicken breasts, skinned and cubed
- 2 tablespoons nam pla (fish sauce)
- 2 tablespoons water
- 2 teaspoons sugar
- 1 red chilli, sliced
- 10 holy or sweet basil leaves
- 4 kaffir lime leaves, shredded
- 125 g (4 oz) roasted cashew nuts (see page 77)

BURNT CHILLI PASTE

- 3 tablespoons groundnut oil
- 1 small red onion, finely chopped
- 6–8 large dried red chillies, finely chopped
- 6 garlic cloves, finely chopped
- 1 tablespoon dried prawns (optional)
- 2 tablespoons nam pla (fish sauce)
- 1 tablespoon tamarind water
- 2 tablespoons brown sugar

TO GARNISH

- 1 red chilli, sliced
- basil sprigs

1 First make the burnt chilli paste. Heat the oil, add the onion and fry until softened. Remove with a slotted spoon and reserve. Add the chillies and fry until blackened, remove and reserve. Add the garlic and fry until golden brown.

2 Grind the prawns, if using, add half of the fried chillies and blend coarsely. Add the onion and garlic and blend to a coarse paste. Add the mixture to the oil with the nam pla, tamarind water and sugar. Heat gently for 2–3 minutes, stirring constantly.

3 Heat the oil in a wok or heavy-based frying pan and fry the sliced garlic until beginning to brown. Add the chicken and fry quickly on all sides. Crumble the remaining fried chillies over the chicken and add 2 tablespoons of the chilli paste, the nam pla, water, sugar and chilli to the pan and stir-fry over a high heat. Add the basil leaves, kaffir lime leaves and cashew nuts and stir-fry for 1 more minute. Garnish with sliced red chilli and basil sprigs.

Serves 4 / **Preparation time** 15 minutes / **Cooking time** 20-25 minutes

crab omelette

kai yat sai poo

- **75 g (3 oz) crab meat**
- **2 eggs**
- **1 heaped teaspoon spring onion greens, finely sliced**
- **¼ onion, chopped**
- **15 g (½ oz) coriander leaves, finely chopped**
- **1 tablespoon nam pla (fish sauce)**
- **4 tablespoons oil**

1 Combine all the ingredients except the oil in a bowl and stir thoroughly.

2 Heat the oil in a wok until it begins to smoke. Empty the contents of the bowl into the wok and turn the heat down to low. The omelette will puff up as it cooks and, after 2–3 minutes, when the underside is brown, turn it over and cook for about another 20 seconds. Fold the omelette in half, slide it on to a plate and serve immediately.

Serves 2 / **Preparation time** 4 minutes / **Cooking time** 3-4 minutes

green papaya salad

som tam

- **375 g (12 oz) green papayas, peeled**
- **2 garlic cloves, crushed**
- **3 red bird chillies, chopped, plus extra to garnish**
- **4 cherry tomatoes**
- **2 tablespoons nam pla (fish sauce)**
- **2 teaspoons caster sugar**
- **juice of 1 lime**
- **1 tablespoon dried shrimp paste**
- **3 tablespoons roasted peanuts, chopped**
- **2 tablespoons roughly chopped coriander leaves, plus extra to garnish**

1 Roughly grate the papaya flesh or cut it into fine shreds.

2 Pound the garlic, chillies and cherry tomatoes to a rough purée using a large pestle and mortar. Add the grated papaya, nam pla, sugar, lime juice and dried shrimp paste and pound together until roughly mixed.

3 Add the chopped peanuts and coriander leaves and serve. Garnish with the extra red bird chillies and coriander leaves.

Tip Green papayas can be found in oriental stores but if you cannot find any use grated carrot or unripe mango instead.

Serves 4 / **Preparation time** 30 minutes

stir-fried squid with basil

pla mook pad grapao

- **2 tablespoons oil**
- **6 garlic cloves, chopped**
- **12 small green chillies, finely sliced**
- **1–2 shallots, chopped**
- **125 g (4 oz) squid, cleaned and cut into strips**
- **½ green pepper, cored, deseeded and chopped**
- **2 tablespoons fish stock**
- **1 tablespoon nam pla (fish sauce)**
- **1 teaspoon palm sugar or light muscovado sugar**
- **15 g (½ oz) basil leaves**
- **finely sliced spring onions tops, to garnish**

1 Heat the oil in a wok, add the garlic, chillies and shallots and fry for 30 seconds. Add the squid and green pepper, turn the heat to high and stir-fry for 1 minute then reduce the heat and add the stock, nam pla, sugar and basil. Cook, stirring, for 1 minute, then serve, garnished with the spring onions.

Serves 4 / **Preparation time** 10 minutes / **Cooking time** about 3 minutes

Serves 4 / **Preparation time** 8-10 minutes, + soaking /
Cooking time 8-10 minutes

vegetable stuffed omelette
kai yat sai

- **1 tablespoon groundnut oil**
- **3 eggs, beaten**
- **salt and pepper, to taste**
- **Crispy Basil (see below), to garnish**

FILLING

- **3 tablespoons groundnut oil**
- **2 garlic cloves, chopped**
- **1 onion, finely chopped**
- **2 tablespoons thin green beans, chopped**
- **2 tablespoons asparagus, chopped**
- **3 baby corn cobs, thinly sliced**
- **1 tomato, diced**
- **4 dried shiitake or exotic mushrooms, soaked, drained, and sliced**
- **1½ teaspoons sugar**
- **2 teaspoons soy sauce**
- **¼ cup water**
- **pinch of salt**

1 First make the filling. Heat the oil in a wok, add the garlic and onion and stir-fry for 30 seconds. Add the beans, asparagus, corn, tomato, mushrooms, sugar and soy sauce and stir-fry for 3–4 minutes, then add the water and salt and continue stir-frying for 2 minutes. Remove the filling from the wok and set aside. Wipe the wok clean with kitchen paper.

2 To make the omelette, heat the oil in the wok, making sure it coats as much of the sides as possible. Pour off any excess. Pour in the beaten eggs, swirling them around in the wok to form a large, thin omelette. Loosen the omelette and move it around with a spatula to make sure it is not sticking to the wok, adding more oil if necessary.

3 When the omelette is almost firm, put the filling in the middle and fold over both sides and ends to form a rectangular parcel, constantly checking that the omelette is not sticking underneath.

4 Carefully remove the omelette from the wok and put it into a serving dish. Serve at once garnished with crispy basil.

Tip To make crispy basil, heat 2 tablespoons groundnut oil in a wok and add 25 g (1 oz) basil leaves and 1 finely sliced small red chilli. Stir-fry for 1 minute until the basil is crispy, then remove with a slotted spoon and drain on kitchen paper.

yellow rice with mushrooms

kao leung gab het

- **2 tablespoons groundnut oil**
- **500 g (1 lb) cold cooked rice**
- **125 g (4 oz) mangetout, trimmed**
- **125 g (4 oz) button mushrooms, halved**
- **125 g (4 oz) canned bamboo shoots, drained**
- **1 teaspoon turmeric**
- **2 teaspoons sugar**
- **1 tablespoon soy sauce**
- **1 teaspoon salt**
- **black pepper, to taste**

TO GARNISH

- **deep-fried garlic slices**
- **1 large fresh red chilli, deseeded and cut into strips**

1 Heat the oil in a wok. Add the rice and stir well, then add all the remaining ingredients and stir-fry over a low heat until thoroughly mixed. Increase the heat and stir and turn for 1–2 minutes, making sure the rice does not stick to the wok.

2 Transfer to a serving dish, garnish with the garlic and chilli and serve immediately.

Serves 4 / **Preparation time** 5 minutes / **Cooking time** 5 minutes

shiitake, bamboo shoot and mangetout stir-fry

pad het, nomai, tualangdao

- **1 tablespoon groundnut oil**
- **2 large garlic cloves, chopped**
- **125 g (4 oz) baby corn cobs, sliced diagonally**
- **10 dried shiitake or exotic mushrooms, soaked, drained, and sliced**
- **125 g (4 oz) canned bamboo shoots, drained**
- **50 g (2 oz) mangetout peas, trimmed**
- **1 teaspoon sugar**
- **3 tablespoons soy sauce**
- **1 tablespoon water**
- **ground black pepper, to taste**

1 Heat the oil in a wok and add the garlic. Stir quickly, then add all the remaining ingredients one at a time. Stir-fry over a high heat for 2–3 minutes, then transfer to a serving dish. Serve immediately.

Serves 4 / **Preparation time** 10 minutes, + soaking / **Cooking time** 3-4 minutes

hot and sour noodle salad

yum gwoideo

- ½ **cucumber, peeled, halved and deseeded**
- **50 g (2 oz) vermicelli rice noodles**
- **1 carrot, cut into long julienne strips**
- **1 red chilli, deseeded and cut intolong julienne strips**
- **2 tablespoons coriander leaves**
- **salt**
- **coriander sprigs, to garnish**

DRESSING

- **2 tablespoons sunflower oil**
- ½ **teaspoon sesame oil**
- **2 teaspoons caster sugar**
- **2 tablespoons lime juice**
- **1 tablespoon nam pla (fish sauce)**
- **salt and pepper**

1 Sprinkle the cucumber with a little salt and set aside to drain for 30 minutes. Cover the noodles in boiling water and soak for 4–6 minutes, or according to the packet instructions. Wash and dry the cucumber and drain and dry the noodles.

2 Combine all the dressing ingredients and season with salt and pepper, to taste. Reserve 2 tablespoons of the dressing and toss the remainder with half the noodles. Place in a large bowl.

3 Cut the cucumber into long thin julienne strips and add to the noodles together with the julienne strips of carrot and chilli. Stir in the coriander and the reserved dressing and serve at once, garnished with coriander sprigs.

Serves 4-6 / **Preparation time** 15 minutes, + draining

basic recipes

soy and vinegar dipping sauce

- **3 tablespoons distilled white vinegar or Chinese rice vinegar**
- **3 tablespoons dark soy sauce**
- **1½ teaspoons caster sugar**
- **2 small fresh red chillies, finely sliced**

1 Combine all the ingredients in a bowl and stir until the sugar has dissolved.

Serves 4
Preparation time 2 minutes

hot sweet sauce

- **100 ml (3½ fl oz) distilled white vinegar or Chinese rice vinegar**
- **65 g (2½ oz) palm sugar or soft brown sugar**
- **¼ teaspoon salt**
- **1 small fresh green chilli, finely chopped**
- **1 small fresh red chilli, finely chopped**

1 Pour the vinegar into a small saucepan and place over a gentle heat. Add the sugar and salt and cook, stirring, until the sugar has dissolved. Remove from the heat and leave to cool.

2 Pour the sauce into a small bowl and stir in the chopped chillies.

Serves 4
Preparation time 5 minutes
Cooking time 1-2 minutes

garlic oil

- **4 tablespoons vegetable oil or sunflower oil**
- **1 tablespoon crushed garlic**

1 Heat the oil in a small frying pan and then add the crushed garlic. Cook slowly over gentle heat until the garlic is golden, stirring occasionally. Use in recipes as required.

Makes 5 tablespoons
Preparation time 3-4 minutes

chilli sauce

- **8 fresh red chillies, chopped**
- **4 garlic cloves, crushed**
- **1 tablespoon nam pla (fish sauce)**
- **2 teaspoons sugar**
- **2 tablespoons lime or lemon juice**
- **¼ teaspoon salt**
- **125 ml (4 fl oz) water**
- **2 tablespoons groundnut oil**

1 Put the chillies, garlic, nam pla, sugar, lime or lemon juice and the salt into a small saucepan. Stir in the water and oil and bring to the boil, then reduce the heat and simmer gently for 10–15 minutes. Blend until smooth in a food processor or blender then transfer to a screw-top jar. This sauce can be stored in the refrigerator for a maximum of 2 weeks. Use as required.

Makes about 150 ml (5 fl oz)
Preparation time 5 minutes
Cooking time 15-20 minutes

plum sauce

- **tablespoons distilled white vinegar or Chinese rice vinegar**
- **4 tablespoons plum jam**
- **1 small fresh red chilli, finely sliced**

1 Put the vinegar and jam into a small saucepan and heat gently, mixing thoroughly.

2 Remove from the heat, turn into a small bowl and leave to cool. Add the sliced fresh chilli before serving.

Serves 4
Preparation time 1 minute
Cooking time 2 minutes

crushed roasted nuts

- **25 g (1 oz) roasted peanuts or cashew nuts**

1 Dry-fry the nuts in a frying pan, without oil. Stir constantly until they turn golden in colour. Remove from the heat and allow to cool.

2 Place the nuts in a plastic bag and break into small pieces using a rolling pin.

3 You can roast and crush any quantity of nuts, then store what you do not need for up to 1 month in an airtight container in the refrigerator.

Makes 25g (1 oz)
Preparation time 4-7 minutes

green curry paste

- **15 small green chillies**
- **4 garlic cloves, halved**
- **2 lemon grass stalks, finely chopped**
- **2 kaffir lime leaves, torn**
- **2 shallots, chopped**
- **50 g (2 oz) coriander leaves, stalks and roots**
- **2.5 cm (1 inch) piece fresh root ginger, peeled and chopped**
- **2 teaspoons coriander seeds**
- **1 teaspoon black peppercorns**
- **1 teaspoon finely grated lime rind**
- **½ teaspoon salt**
- **2 tablespoons groundnut oil**

1 Put all the ingredients in a food processor or blender and grind to a thick paste.

2 Transfer the paste to an airtight container. Any that you do not use immediately may be stored in the refrigerator for up to 3 weeks.

Preparation time 15 minutes

red curry paste

- **6 dried red chillies, deseeded, soaked and roughly chopped**
- **2 tablespoons chopped lemon grass**
- **1 teaspoon chopped coriander root or stem**
- **1 tablespoon chopped shallots**
- **1 tablespoon chopped garlic**
- **1 teaspoon chopped galangal**
- **2 teaspoons coriander seeds**
- **1 teaspoon cumin seeds**
- **6 white peppercorns**
- **1 teaspoon salt**
- **1 teaspoon shrimp paste**

1 Put all the curry paste ingredients into a food processor and grind to a thick paste.

2 Transfer the paste to an airtight container. Any that you do not use immediately may be stored in the refrigerator for up to 3 weeks.

Preparation time 15 minutes

yellow curry paste

- **3 small fresh yellow/orange chillies**
- **4 garlic cloves, chopped**
- **4 shallots, roughly chopped**
- **3 teaspoons turmeric**
- **1 teaspoon salt**
- **15 black peppercorns**
- **1 lemon grass stalk, finely chopped**
- **2.5 cm (1 inch) piece fresh root ginger, chopped**
- **1 teaspoon ground coriander**
- **1 teaspoon ground cumin**
- **1 teaspoon shrimp paste**

1 Put all the curry paste ingredients into a food processor and grind to a thick paste.

2 Transfer the paste to an airtight container. Any that you do not use immediately may be stored in the refrigerator for up to 3 weeks.

Makes 150 ml (¼ pint)
Preparation time 15 minutes

tamarind sauce

- **150 ml (¼ pint) tamarind juice**
- **125 g (4 oz) demerara sugar**
- **2 tablespoons nam pla (fish sauce)**

1 Put the tamarind juice into a saucepan and add the sugar and nam pla. Bring to the boil and simmer, stirring occasionally, until the sugar has dissolved and the sauce is thick.

Makes 150 ml (1/4 pint)
Preparation time 5 minutes

garlic mixture

- **2 tablespoons crushed garlic**
- **2 tablespoons chopped coriander roots or stalks**
- **½ tablespoon pepper**

1 Put all the ingredients into a mortar and grind with a pestle until they are thoroughly blended and form a paste. If you like, garlic mixture can be made in advance and stored, covered, in the refrigerator for 1–2 days until required. This will enhance the flavour.

Preparation time 5 minutes

coconut cream and milk

- **400 g (13 oz) grated or desiccated coconut**
- **900 ml (1½ pints) milk**

1 Mix the coconut and milk together in a saucepan. Bring to the boil then lower the heat and simmer, stirring, until the mixture is reduced by one-third. Strain, pressing the mixture against the sides of the sieve to extract as much liquid as possible.

2 Pour the strained coconut milk into a bowl and chill in the refrigerator. When it is really cold, skim off the thicker 'cream' that rises to the surface. The remaining liquid is the coconut milk.

Preparation time 10 minutes

sticky rice

- **500 g (I lb) glutinous rice**

1 Put the rice into a large bowl, cover with plenty of cold water and leave to soak overnight.

2 Drain the rice and place in a steamer lined with muslin or a double thickness of kitchen paper. Place over a pan of boiling water and steam for 30 minutes, covered.

3 Remove the heat and leave to stand for 10 minutes then turn out on to a tray and break up any lumps with a spatula. Place the rice in a covered container until ready to serve. To eat, pull off pieces of rice and mould them in your hand.

Serves 4-6
Preparation time 5 minutes
Cooking time 30 minutes

easy satay sauce

- **1 tablespoon groundnut oil**
- **2 teaspoons Red Curry Paste (see page 78)**
- **3 tablespoons coconut milk**
- **125 ml (4 fl oz) water**
- **3 tablespoons palm sugar or light muscovado sugar**
- **125 g (4 oz) peanuts, crushed**

1 Heat the oil in a wok, add the curry paste and stir over a gentle heat for 30 seconds, then add all the remaining ingredients. Stir well and cook over a moderate heat for 10–15, stirring occasionally. Add a little more water if you feel the sauce is becoming too thick. To serve, turn the sauce into a small bowl.

Serves 4
Preparation time 5 minutes
Cooking time 15-17 minutes

index

Picture credits
Octopus Publishing Group Ltd./Sandra Lane 4 left, 4
right, 5 right, 6 left, 6 right, 6 Centre, 7 left, 8 left, 9, 9
left, 9 Centre, 13, 15, 17, 20, 21, 25, 29, 33, 39, 44, 49,
50, 59, 62, 73, 74 /David Loftus title, 8 Centre, 10-11,
16, 26, 34, 46, 60, 65, 66-67, 68, 70, 77, 79 /Neil Mersh
7 Right, 35 /James Murphy 36 /Peter Myers 7 Centre,
8 right, 19, 24, 43, 52, 58 /Philip Webb 5 left, 55